CLASSICS TO MODERNS
IN THE EARLY-ADVANCED GRADES

Compiled and Edited by Denes Agay

FOREWORD

This collection of fifty-four original piano works is a sequel to our previously published and now widely used three volumes in the "Classics To Moderns" series (Music for Millions Nos. 17, 27 and 37). The piano literature of nearly three centuries is represented by these compositions in the early-advanced grades. The titles follow an approximately chronological sequence from the Baroque to our modern period. All selections are in their original form, neither rearranged, nor simplified, and are based on Urtext or other highly reliable editions. Fingering marks were added and long appogiaturas were written out by the editor. Tempo indications in the works of the 17th and early 18th century are also editorial suggestions, as are all dynamic and expression marks set in parentheses. The French tempo marks of the Couperin pieces are, of course, by the composer.

We hope that this latest addition to the "Classics To Moderns" family of books will be as useful and inspiring as have been its companion volumes in this, by now universally recognized, piano series.

Order Number: AM 41674
International Standard Book Number: 0.8256.4047.4
Library of Congress Catalog Card Number: 78-83972

Exclusive Distributors:
Music Sales Corporation
257 Park Avenue South, New York, NY 10010 USA
Music Sales Limited
8/9 Frith Street, London W1V 5TZ England
Music Sales Pty. Limited
120 Rothschild Street, Rosebery, Sydney, NSW 2018, Australia

Printed in the United States of America by
Vicks Lithograph and Printing Corporation

Amsco Publications
London/New York/Sydney

CONTENTS

COMPOSERS' INDEX

Prelude

from Suite No. 5

Henry Purcell

*All tempo and dynamic marks printed in small type are editorial suggestions.

La Linotte Effarouchée

The Startled Bird

François Couperin

La Bandoline

Legerement, sans vitesse (Lightly, not fast)

François Couperin

2nd Couplet

Sonata

(L. 104)

Allegro

Domenico Scarlatti

Sonata
(L. 90)

Allegro

Domenico Scarlatti

14

L'Egyptienne

Jean Philippe Rameau

19

Sinfonia 7
(Three - Voice Invention)

Johann Sebastian Bach

Praeludium 21

from "The Well-Tempered Clavier", Part 1

Johann Sebastian Bach

Vivace

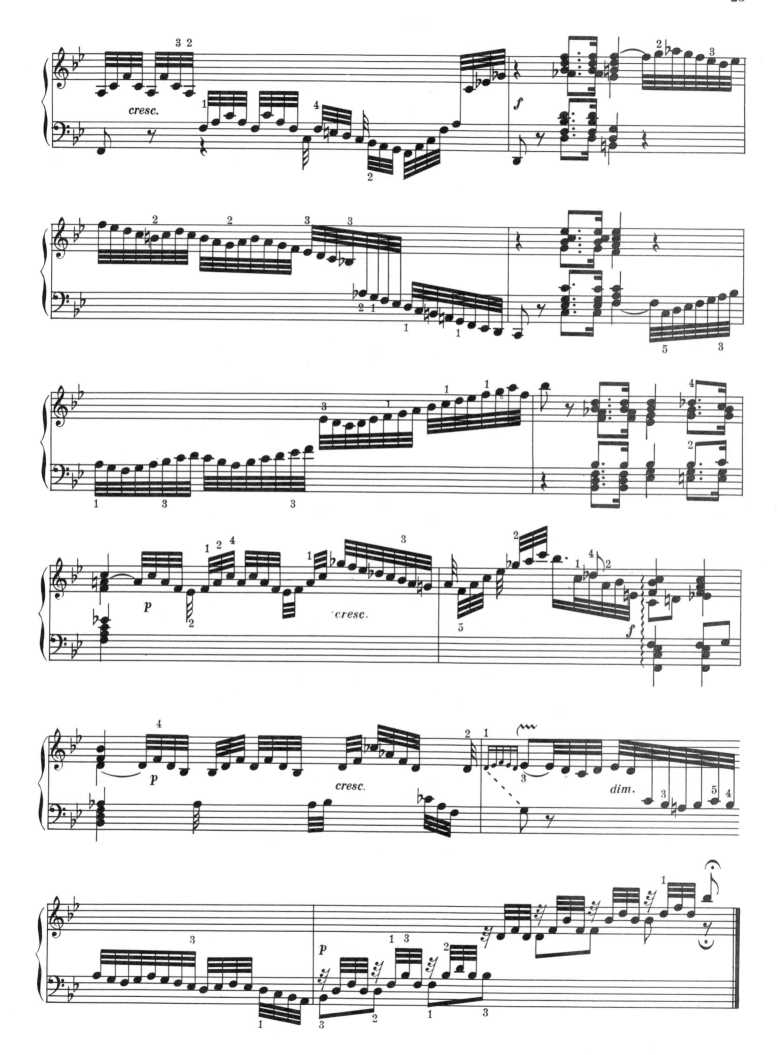

Fuga 21

from "The Well-Tempered Clavier", Part 1

Johann Sebastian Bach

Rondeaux

from Partita No. 2

Johann Sebastian Bach

Echo
from the "French Overture"

Johann Sebastian Bach

✽ All dynamic marks, with the exception of the two in parenthesis, are by Bach

Fantasia

Georg Philipp Telemann

D.C. al Fine

Gigue

from Suite No. 4

George Frideric Handel

Air and Variations

from Suite No. 1, Book 2

George Frideric Handel

Andantino

Variation 1

Allegretto

Variation 2
Più mosso

Variation 3

Variation 4

Variation 5

Presto

Ouverture
from a Suite in G minor

George Frideric Handel

✳ *all eighth notes may be played staccato*

Allegro Assai
from a Sonata in D minor

Carl Philipp Emanuel Bach

Presto

from Sonata No.40

Joseph Haydn

Tempo Di Menuetto

Finale from Sonata No. 22

Joseph Haydn

Two German Dances
1

Edited by Denes Agay

Ludwig van Beethoven

2

Bagatelle

Ludwig van Beethoven

Trio

D.C.

Sonata*

K.312

Wolfgang Amadeus Mozart

* *This work consists of only one movement*

Andante Con Variazioni

from Sonata No. 12, Op. 26

Ludwig van Beethoven

Variation 1

Variation 2

Variation 3

Variation 4

Variation 5

Two Ländler

Franz Schubert

Impromtu

Op. 142 No. 2

Franz Schubert

Allegretto

sempre legato

Fantasie
(K.397)

Wolfgang Amadeus Mozart

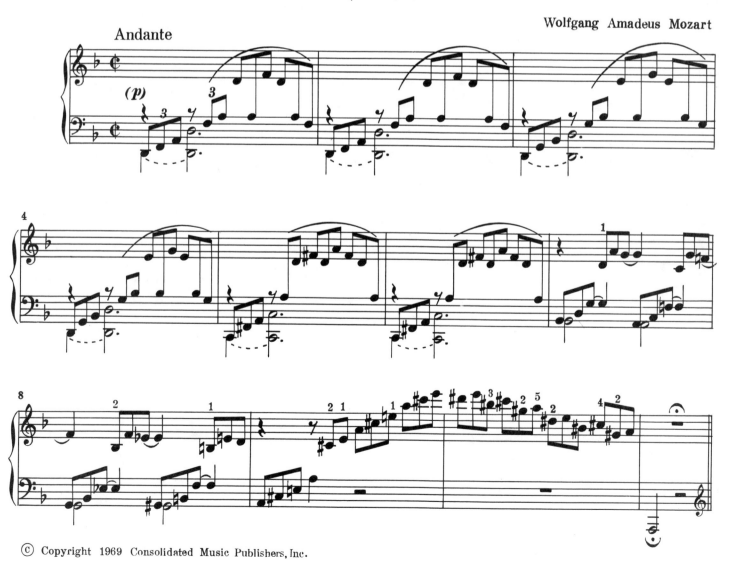

Adagio

Tempo primo

Moment Musical

Op. 94 No. 5

Franz Schubert

Allegro vivace

Song Without Words

Op.102, No.4

Felix Mendelssohn - Bartholdy

Song Without Words

Op. 102, No.3

Felix Mendelssohn-Bartholdy

Fantasy Piece

Op. 111 No. 3

Robert Schumann

Kräftig und sehr markiert (♩ = 96)
(Vigorously, with very marked rhythm)

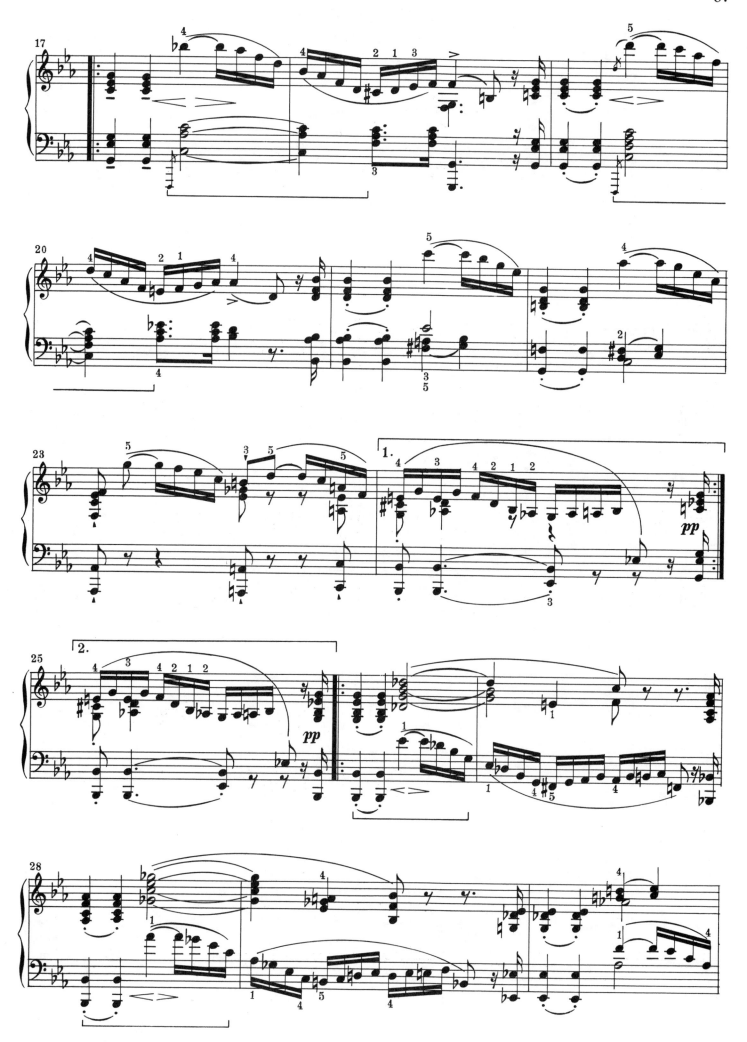

Friendly Landscape

from "Waldscenen" Op.82, No.5

Robert Schumann

Romanze

from "Faschingsschwank aus Wien" Op.26, No.2

Robert Schumann

Ziemlich langsam (Rather slow) ♪ = 92

The Elf
Op.127 No.17

So schnell als möglich
(As fast as possible)

Robert Schumann

Waltz
Op. 70, No. 2

Frédéric Chopin

Tempo giusto

Nocturne

Op.32, No.1

Frédéric Chopin

Appassionato

Franz Liszt

Two Waltzes

Op. 39 No's. 1.2.

1.

Tempo giusto

Johannes Brahms

2.

Intermezzo

Op. 118 No. 2

Johannes Brahms

Valse - Scherzo

Op.59 No.2

Allegro in tempo di Valse

Peter I. Tchaikovsky

Conversation Piece

Op. 85, No. 11

Antonin Dvořák

* trill on B♭

Humoreske

Op. 61, No. 2

Edvard Grieg

Tempo di Minuetto ed energico

Scherzino

"Ballet Of Unhatched Chickens"
from "Pictures From An Exhibition"

Modest P. Mussorgsky

Once Upon A Time

Op. 44 No. 3

Max Reger

Moderately slow and expressive

Scotch Poem

Op. 31, No. 2

Edward MacDowell

Allegro tempestoso

Prelude
Op. 11 No. 16

Alexander Skriabin

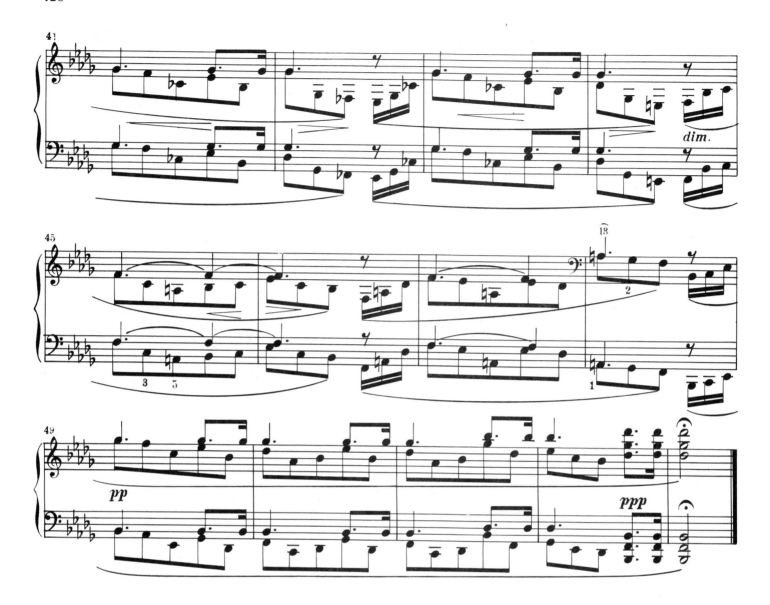

Album Leaf

Op. 2, No. 4

Bedřich Smetana

Spanish Dance

"Minueto" from "Danzas Espanoles", Op.5

Enrique Granados

Postludium

from " Winterreigen" Op.13

Ernö von Dohnányi

Allegro non troppo

Clair De Lune

from "Suite Bergamasque"

Andante très expressif

Claude Debussy

pp   con sordina

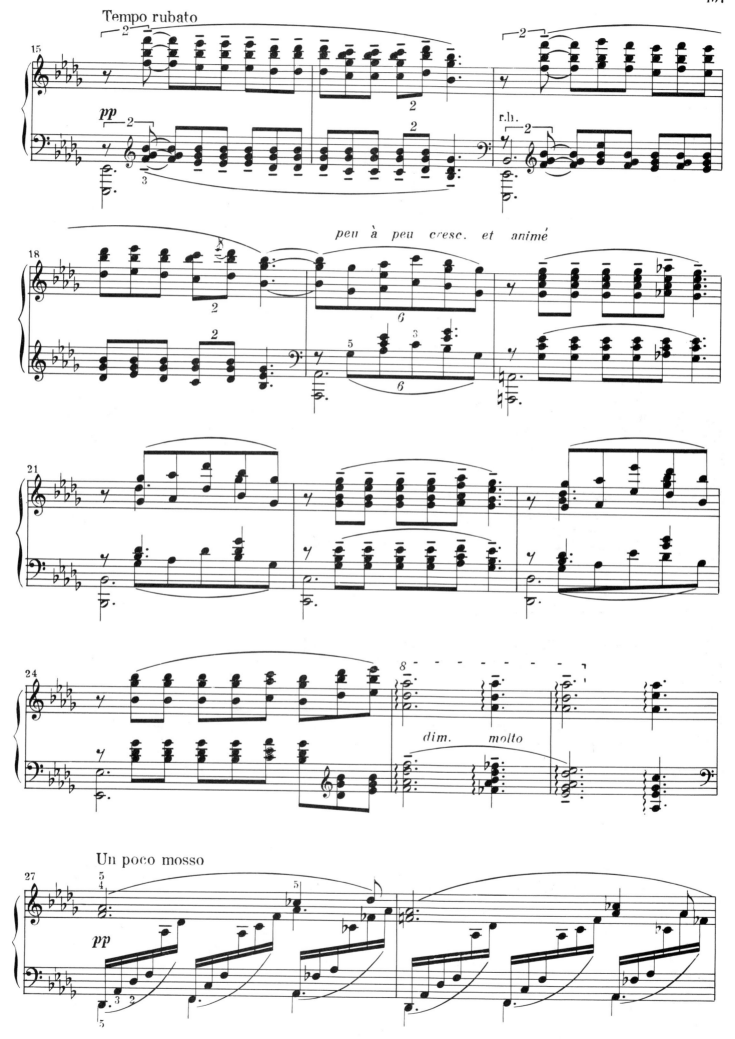

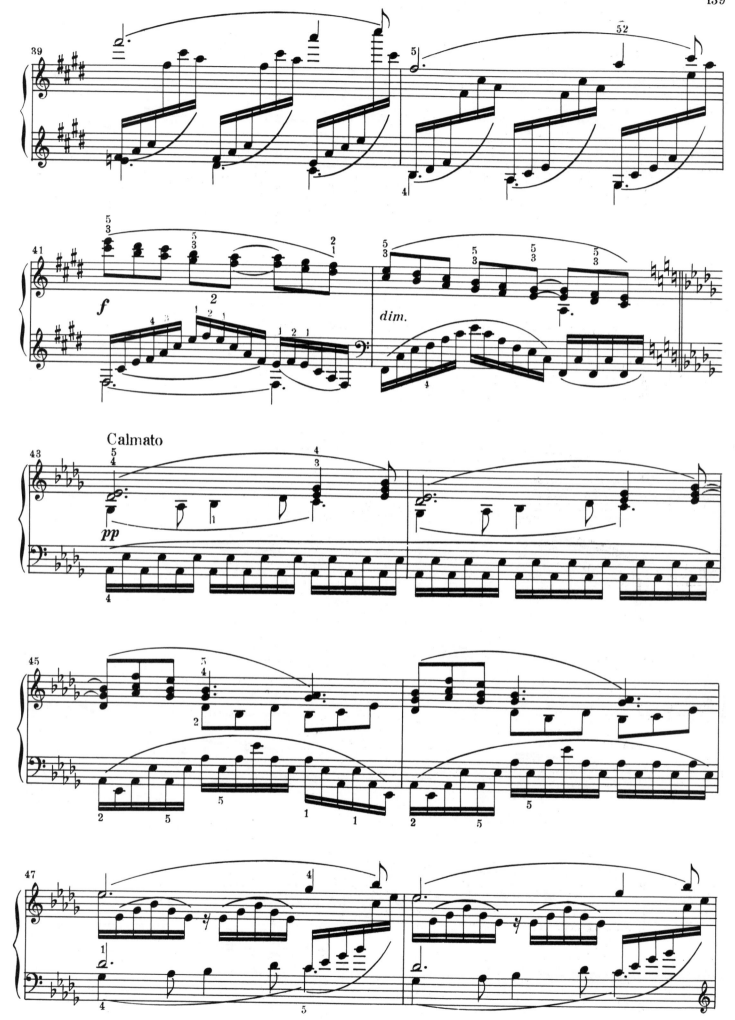

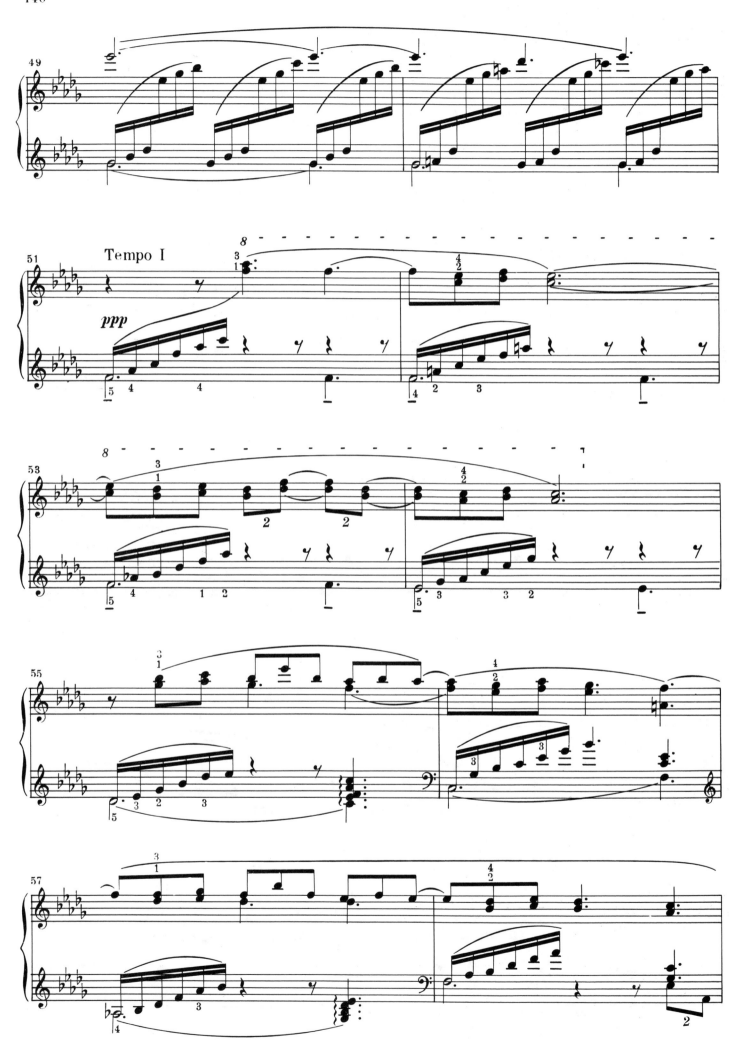

First Arabesque

Claude Debussy

Tempo rubato (poco meno mosso)

Menuet
from Sonatine

Maurice Ravel

Mouv^t de Menuet (Tempo di Minuetto)

Gavotte

Op 32, No.3

Serge Prokofieff

Fantastic Dance
No. 3

Allegretto

Dmitri Shostakovich

Prelude

Op. 38, No. 2

Dmitri Kabalevsky

Scherzando (Allegro moderato)

Armenian Dance

Aram Khatchaturian

To next strain

To Fine

Fine

con Ped.

D.C. al Fine

Bagatelle
Op.6 No.2

Béla Bartók

See-Saw

from "Seven Sketches," Op.9

Béla Bartók

Commodo